Legal Disclosures

Table of Contents

COVID19 Effects On American Real Estate

About the Author

Victor is a Real Estate Investor, Developer & Investment Manager born in Lagos Nigeria, based in Atlanta Ga USA who started out his investing career in 2012. He obtained his Bachelors of Business Administration degree in Finance and is the Founder of conglomerate firm Zirowin Group. Our portfolio includes Zirow Invest LLC, Zirowin Capital (Real Estate Development & Investment Management), OFFERVEST (Home Buying Firm).

Collectively his business portfolio has acquired and closed over $4M dollars worth over real estate & been a keystone in closing 50+ investment deals with investors. He has been featured in notable publications such as Forbes Magazine, Black Enterprise & was nominated for Rice Awards business person of the year in 2018. His group of companies specializes in the acquisitions, financial analysis, development, and reselling of residential and commercial investment properties. He also has extensive experience working with investors of all ranges (domestic & international) from new investors, all the way up to multi-million dollar private equity hedge funds. The asset types he specializes in are Single Family Homes, Land, & Multifamily properties. He values building relationships and doing business with integrity, while executing and closing deals on a very high level.

His personal mission statement is: to be an inspiration to the world, to empower people to pursue their passions, embrace their journey, and follow their dreams.

Victor E. Bomi

Introduction

I value creating life-long relationships with people and enjoy being able to help families accomplish their financial goals. Business, finance, and investing are my personal passions and I believe everyone is capable of accomplishing financial freedom if they are provided the right guidelines and resources.

I've worked my way up and learned a lot through my real estate investing experiences since 2012, invested thousands into successful industry mentors for my own personal growth in life & real estate, and am happy to share some of what I have learned with you. By the end of this book, you will have a firm foundation to begin or expand on real estate investing in America whether you are a domestic or international investor. Thank you for your support & enjoy the first edition of Investing In American Real Estate +

PURPOSE: The overall purpose of this book is to pull back the complicated curtains of American real estate investing and provide you with the clear guidelines and foundations needed to be able to successfully invest in American real estate whether you are based in America or in another country.

WHO THIS BOOK IS FOR: This book is for those who are looking to achieve financial freedom through real estate investing, build upon already established wealth, for international investors who are interested in acquiring property in America, and for real estate investors who are interested in navigating through the Covid 19 Market successfully.

WHY YOU SHOULD INVEST IN REAL ESTATE: Historically, real estate investing has created the most millionaires in the world out of any asset class and is the #1 way to achieve financial freedom to provide a legacy & financial security for your loved ones.

Getting Started Investing In Real Estate

Types of Real Estate Investing Strategies to Consider:

Passive Investing & Private Lending

Buy, Fix, & Sell (Rehabbing)

Buy, Fix, & Hold (Rentals)

Buy, Rehab, Rent, Refinance (BRRR)

New Construction & Land Developments

Turnkey Rentals (Cashflowing Properties)

House Hacking

Wholetailing

Wholesaling (Contract Flipping)

Investment Strategies (Breakdown)

Passive Investing & Private Lending: Lending your capital to an active developer and investor who has the experience and resources to find great deals - they do the work, you get paid. **Key Benefits:** This is the simplest way to make money in real estate. See anywhere from 8-15% in returns. Won't have to deal with headaches of tenants, managing contractors, looking for deals, etc. Your money is secured by the property, insurance, and a deed of trust contract. **Time Factor:** You are paid monthly or when the deal closes

Buy, Fix, Sell (Rehabbing): The process of buying, renovating, and re-selling a property. If you have a big risk tolerance and are patient enough to wait for your pay-day then this is the strategy for you. This investment model is a very risky & cash-heavy strategy (even if you're being financed) you will still need to account for your 20% down-payment, closing costs and holding costs (mortgage interest, taxes, insurance, utilities, maintenance). You will also have to know how to deal with and manage contractors and have general knowledge about construction so you are not cheated by your contractor. **Key Benefits:** You usually get really good deals (properties sold at discount), when done right most rehabs yield 5 figure profits. **Time Factor:** It takes **3-6 months** to complete a rehab & sell depending on the extent of renovation & your contractor

Turnkey Rentals: This investment strategy involves acquiring properties that are already fully renovated and are rent ready. **Key Benefit:** they are usually already cash flowing with a tenant and property management in place. The only major downside is that they are usually priced a lot more expensive and closer to retail. So if you're willing to pay that premium price in exchange for everything already being in place - then go for it, just be sure to do your due diligence on the tenant and property management company. **Time Factor:** depends on if you're a cash buyer or being financed - **7 days vs. 45 days**.

Buy Fix & Hold: The alternative to turnkey rentals is to simply buy, fix, and hold. We personally prefer this model for rentals for our investors. **Key Benefits:** you are in more control as the investor (over the quality of the rehab, the quality of your tenants) and get a much better return on investment because most buy, fix and hold deals are sold at a discounted price. (You still need to be sure to have cash reserves for expenses)

Investment Strategies (Breakdown)

House Hacking

When you buy a small multi-unit - usually a 2-4 unit property, live on-site in one of the units, and rent out the remaining vacant units. **Key Benefits:** This is a great way to start building passive income & begin your real estate portfolio, you can usually implement this strategy via an FHA Loan, that requires a low down-payment (3.5%) + 580 Credit Score to get qualified. **Time Factor:** depends on your lender, their underwriting process, and how fast you are able to get approved for the loan - but usually this process can take anywhere from **45-60 days.**

Investment Strategies (Breakdown)

Buy, Rehab, Rent, Refinance (BRRR)

This strategy refers to acquiring a property (at the right price - a discount), then renovating it to make it habitable for a tenant, sourcing a qualified tenant to rent the property, then refinancing the property with a lender. The key to successfully implementing this strategy is to be sure you bought the property at a good enough discount **(70%)** to where there is a lot of built-in equity and are able to cash-out refinance with your lender **(pull cash out against the appraised value of your property minus the original loan + closing costs and refinance your original loan to get better rates)** to then turn around and repeat this process in another property with the cash you just pulled out. You will usually have to wait via a "seasoning period" in order to qualify for the cash-out refi with most lenders.

Summary: This strategy is essentially just a creative way for financing (replacing a short-term loan with a long-term one) and acquiring rentals while taking back out the initial cash outlay you put in to acquire the property in the first place.

KEY BENEFITS
- One of the best ways to build a large real estate portfolio
- Opportunity to use leverage
- Interest rates on re-fis are lower than other forms of debt and loans
- The cash you pull out is tax-free
- This is a great strategy to use in both residential and commercial real estate (Apartments).

KEY RISKS
- Property may not appraise for the price you need to get cash-out (very important)
- Negative cash flow or no cashflow at all due to property being vacant
- 6-12 months seasoning period
- Usually, you finance the rehab costs with your own money or cash
- Overleveraging is a risk here - be careful

KEY POINTS TO REMEMBER

- Most lenders will refinance up to 75% of the Retail Value
- You should keep all your costs (purchase price + rehab cost) to be less than 70% of the Retail Value when buying in order to successfully implement this strategy
- Don't miscalculate your retail value (very important - (you don't want a situation where your property appraises for less than what you're borrowing against
- You pay closing costs on the entire loan amount of your new loan
- Don't forget to account for holding costs
- Maintain a large flow of Cash Reserves (in case of emergency)

BRRR DEAL EXAMPLE

$100,000 - Purchase Price (includes 1st closing costs)
$20,000 - Down Payment (20%)
$80,000 - Original Loan
$15,000 - Renovation Cost + Holding Cost
$2,000 - Re-Fi Closing Costs (2nd closing costs)
$200,000 - Appraised Valued

You purchase the property for $100k, put down $20k to your hard money lender, your lender finances the remaining $80k balance, you then renovate the property for $15k, rent it out for $1k/month, then wait 6 months for "the required seasoning period" to refinance at 75% of the Appraised Value - the property the appraised for $200k

$150,000 (75% of Appraised Value)

Refinance and Pay off your original loan of $80,000 + $2,000 refi closing costs, this leaves you with $68,000. Take your $68,000 and find another property and repeat the BRRR process again

Your Total Cash Out of Pocket: $20k + $15k = $35k (you get that back) in the $68k (while you enjoy your monthly income from the $1k/month)

Investment Strategies (Breakdown)

Wholesaling: the process of locating a property owner that is interested in selling their property (and willing to sell their property to you at a heavily discounted rate to the retail value of the property) you make an offer to the owner via a purchase contract to buy their property at an agreed-upon price - then you turn around and sell your contract at a higher price to a cash buyer investor who is looking for discounted deals like the one you have. **Key Benefits:** If you have ever wanted to invest in real estate but don't have the capital or credit to do so, then this is the strategy for you. **Time Factor:** These transactions normally take anywhere from **7-30 days** - it's a great way to make of a lot of cash in a relatively short amount of time (wholesale fees range from $5k-$30k+ | Wholesaling is a very **Time-Intensive** business model, so if you don't have the time to invest into building the business, finding property owners who want to sell, finding cash buyers, etc then I would advise against it.

Wholesale Deal Example:
123 Main Street, Atlanta Ga, US, 30310
Retail Value of Property: $250,000
Property Repair Cost: $70,000
You and seller agree to $70k price
You get a signed contract to buy for $70k
You find a cash buyer for $80k
You assign your interests in your original $70k contract for $10k to your cash buyer - **You just made $10k**

Wholetailng: the process of buying a property that doesn't need much repairs but standard cosmetic updates (paint, carpet, kitchen, lights, landscaping) at a discounted price to the retail value and performing those updates, and turning around and re-selling it at a discount on the open market. For you to execute this strategy well, you have to be sure to buy the property at a discount, not over-rehab it, and not over-price it too close to the retail value when you get ready to re-sell it to the next buyer. You will likely sell this quickly on the open market because the next buyer is also getting a great deal from you + a property that has been updated. **Key Benefits:** You can make a larger profit doing this strategy than you would make just wholesaling a property, you have full control of the property and not under any pressure to re-sell your contract to a cash buyer, time works for you in this scenario and not against you. **Time Factor:** you can normally close these transactions anywhere from **30-60 days**.

Wholetail Deal Example:
213 Main Street, Atlanta Ga, US, 30310
Retail Value of Property: $250,000
Property Repair Cost: $15,000
You and seller agree to $70k price
You buy & close on the property at $70k
You perform a light cosmetic renovation for $15,000
You re-sell it for $140,000 on the open market via an agent
You will gross $55,000 in profit (minus selling expenses)

Investment Strategies (Breakdown)

New Construction & Land Development

This is the process of identifying and procuring a plot of vacant land (developed or undeveloped) for the purposes of building a new structure on it. Most times a builder, architect, surveyor are just some of the people that would be involved in this process as well. When deciding to build a property (if you are working with a builder) you will usually have two options: A Custom Home - homes in which you design from scratch, you decide all the features of the home vs. Production Home - you will decide on a set of already made plans - that sometimes still allow certain aspects of it to be customized. **Time Factor:** new construction custom homes usually take **10-16 months**, and new construction production homes usually take **6-8 months.** Remember to pay close attention to the zoning regulations for your land, to know what type of structure can be built there and make sure that permits have been pulled for construction work.

Key Benefits: Most times these types of projects are usually already sold before the actual development is complete - so if you are coming in as an investor that is doing a new construction project you have the option to sell your project "Off Plans" - the architectural designs. The primary benefit of doing land development deals is that the profits on these are usually in the 6-figure range (buy the land at the right price and implement cost control in the development phase, and are selling during the right market)

Key Factors That Affect Home Building Timeline

- The Size & Type of Home
- Technicalities of Your Development Plans
- Construction Style (custom or production)
- Builders & Availability of Sub-Contractors
- Weather
- City & City Planning
- Pre-Construction (clearing the lot, removal of trees, rocks etc., rough grading and leveling of foundation)
- Permits (can take 1-3 months)
- Change Orders

New Construction Deal Example:
 0 Main Street, Kennesaw Ga, US, 30144
Retail Value of Property: $600,000
0.7 Acres Land
Building: 4 bed 3 bathroom 2 car garage + 3000 sqft Home

Land Acquisition Cost: $100,000
Building Cost: $330,000 ($100/sqft)
Holding Cost: $20,000 (taxes, insurance, maintenance, utilities, interest)
Resale Price: $600,000

You will gross $150,000 in profit (minus selling expenses)

Types Of Real Assets to Consider

Deciding which type of asset class to invest in depends on a wide range of things such as your personal investment goals, trying to make quick cash? cashflow long term? how much cash do you have available to invest? your risk tolerance? how much time do you have to devote to it?

Residential: Easier to enter the market, lower capital requirement, 15-30 year loans, Family and Individual tenants, higher tenant turnover rate, performs better in economic crisis, value based on equity build up, retail value & income easier to lease (shelter is a basic human need), larger pool of buyers, deals close 7-45 days, deals are easier to analyze, properties are easier to manage

Commercial: Higher barrier to entry, more capital required to get started, loans range from 5-20 years, Corporate (Anchor) tenants, lower turnover-rate, at high risk during an economic crisis, easier to increase value, value mostly based on income and projected income, easier to get financing, smaller pool of buyers when reselling, deals can take months to close, much more complex under-writing and analysis is required, property management more complex

Both asset types can provide you with great returns and long-term wealth, cash-flow, and great tax breaks.

RESIDENTIAL ASSETS

Properties ranging from 1-4 units.

- SINGLE FAMILY HOMES (1 Unit)
- DUPLEX (2-Units)
- TRIPLEX (3-Units)
- QUAD (4-UNITS)
- Townhomes
- Condos

COMMERCIAL ASSETS

Any property with 5 units or more is considered a commercial asset.

- Multi-Family (Apartment Complexes)
- Office Building
- Hotels
- Industrial Building
- Retail
- Healthcare
- Mix-Use
- Land

Key Team Members Needed

> "Teamwork makes Your Dreamwork"
> -Victor

- Lender (if you're not paying cash)

- Agent (to resell your properties)

- Licensed General Contractor (to renovate your properties)

- Project Manager (to manage your contractors & projects)

- Deal Supplier (someone to provide you discounted properties)

- CPA / Accountant

- Closing Attorney / Title Company

- Insurance Agent

- Investment Manager (comprehensive investment plan, deal analyst, economic & market analysis)

- Property Manager

Top Factors to Consider Before Investing

- Your Budget
- The Location & Market
- Resources Available In Your Target Market
- Economic Factors
- Property Condition Factors
- Demographic Factors

Top Factors to Consider Before Investing (Breakdown)

YOUR BUDGET

Median home values change from state to state (In Atlanta Georgia - the average price for a property is $299,000, in Los Angeles it is, $752,000, in Austin Texas, it is $401,000 - via Zillow.com) so when you decide to enter a market you have to be sure to make sure that your budget to invest in that market is enough to get you in the game in that particular market. I always advise clients to **have at least 30% of the median home values' average price** in the form of cash. So in Atlanta for example, you should aim to have at least $100k in cash to invest in our market. A lot of times you will be able to get financing to finance your acquisition if you have the downpayment capital available. (we will go over the financing aspect of investing later on in the book).

RESOURCES AVAILABLE IN YOUR TARGET MARKET

This goes back to having a team and established relationships in the market you are investing in. This is a very important aspect of real estate investing, and can actually make or break you. **One bad contractor** who decides to over-charge you, not finish the work, or extend the timeline can mess up your projected profits, or **a bad agent** who is only worried about a commission rather than your ROI will sell you a bad investment deal. If you are entering a market you need to already be building your network of contacts and relationships in that market, and be sure that the people whom you work with are vetted, qualified professionals with the references and track record to support their work. Personally, one of the things that has helped me do well in real estate has always been working with the right people and having a great team of agents, contractors, lawyers, and industry stakeholders that allow us to successfully do good business.

THE LOCATION & MARKET

"Location, Location, Location" - is a common phrase in our industry to emphasize the importance of choosing the right market when deciding to invest in real estate. The quality of the amenities in the market you're interested in, such as **school ratings** (top school district in Georgia is the Gwinnett School of Mathematics, Science, & Technology in Gwinnett County), and proximity to employment location, hospitals, airports, and proximity to recreational activities like movies, golf courses, and other forms of entertainment. **Median home values** and what properties are selling for in the area are important - and are values trending up or down?

Another factor to consider is the transportation infrastructure set up by the market (public buses? train system? how close are they to your subject property?). Factors that can negatively impact your property's location and value include: foreclosures, vacant boarded-up homes on the same street as your property, a residential property located close to commercial properties, the property is adjacent to a very busy roadway (with double yellow lines). You also have to pay attention to future major developmental plans of the city in which your property is located in and pay attention to key **Fortune 500** companies relocating their headquarters to your potential investment's location (these 2 factors can drastically increase the value of your property). **Pride of Ownership:** Are the other property owners in the neighborhood maintaining their homes? keeping up with the landscaping, exterior paint, etc?

There are a host of other factors to consider but in summary be sure to do your research on the location of your investment & whats going on in the city (and neighborhood, before investing there).

Top Factors to Consider Before Investing (Economic)

UNDERSTANDING REAL ESTATE - MARKET CYCLES

The real estate market by nature is cyclical - it goes up, it goes down. A successful investor, buys at the bottom of the market and sells at the top of the market and is always aware of the best investment strategy to use, depending on the market conditions.

Image Source: Mortgage Sandbox

Phase 1: **Recovery**	Phase 2: **Expansion**	Phase 3: **Hypersupply**	Phase 4: **Recession**
Seller's Market	Seller's Market	Buyer's Market	Buyer's Market
Decreasing vacancy Low construction rates Low rental rate growth Moderate absorption	Decreasing Vacancy Mod/High construction rates Mod/high rental rate growth Moderate absorption	Increasing Vacancy Mod/High construction rates Mod/low rental rate growth Low absorption	Increasing Vacancy Low construction rates Low/neg rental rate growth Low absorption

Shupilov, Y (2018). 4 Phases Of The Real Estate Cycle, Explained. Retrieved from https://news.shupilov.com/blog/4-phases-of-the-real-estate-cycle-explained-investment-strategies/

Top Factors to Consider Before Investing (Economic)

The great thing about investing in the US is that a lot of this data is readily available online, alternatively, your investment advisor or an agent can get you this information.

- ✓ Employment Rate
- ✓ Avg. Salary (Wages)
- ✓ Interest Rates
- ✓ Gross Domestic Product (GDP)
- ✓ Government Policy, Subsidies & Laws
- ✓ New Construction Home Trends (Monthly vs. Yearly)
- ✓ Manufacturing Activity
- ✓ Appreciation Potential

- ✓ Population Size + Population Growth Rate
- ✓ Median Home Values
- ✓ Median (Market) Rent (cash-flow potential)
- ✓ Supply & Demand
- ✓ Vacancy Rates
- ✓ Avg. Age of Property Owners (in area)
- ✓ Avg. Ratio of Renter to Owner (in area)

Top Factors to Consider Before Investing (Property Condition)

PROPERTY CONDITION

You generally want to know the **age & overall condition** of any property you are thinking of investing in. The older a property is, the more likely it will need a complete renovation overhaul (for example the inner city properties in the city of Atlanta were mostly built in the 1960s and some as early as the 1920s - these homes typically need a lot more work **updating plumbing & electrical systems** when it comes to renovations to update their mechanical systems to today's standards (which in turn will result in a higher renovation budget (compared to newer homes built 1980 or newer). **Weather Pattern Risk:** In LA, you have to consider earthquakes, in New Orleans - flooding, in Florida Hurricanes..etc - know the climate patterns of where you are investing). You typically will want to take a licensed general contractor with you to give you a thorough estimate and itemized scope of work on what types of updating the house needs. (I personally recommend you **take at least 3 contractors** and get 3 different bids on each project you are interested in) and be on the lookout for any hidden problems if the house was previously renovated by another contractor.

The roof is another big renovation job to look out for, that usually costs tens of thousands to fix **(You should replace your roof every 10-15 years)** A property with a bad foundation for us is a deal killer, these usually tend to be more of a headache than they're worth - so you should be sure to note any structural problems when inspecting the property. **(sloping floors / un-even flooring, cracks internally on the walls & externally on the bottom sides of the property - these are signs of foundation issues)**

"THE BIG 5" - You Should Always Pay Attention To In A Property

- ✓ ELECTRICAL SYSTEM
- ✓ PLUMBING SYSTEM
- ✓ HEATING & AIR SYSTEM
- ✓ ROOF
- ✓ FOUNDATION

Take note of the age of the appliance systems in the property (if any of the following items are **more than 15 years old** it may be time to replace them: washer, dryer, refrigerators, water heater, furnaces, and central air system)

Property Floor Plan & Non-Modern Features: most homes of today have open floor plans and island kitchens, in older homes there tends to be walled off rooms, out-dated updates, very low and uncomfortable ceilings, in-efficient windows & insulation (that will drive up your energy bill)

Pay attention to the material the house was made out of brick, stucco, pre-fab, etc. & whether the property was a production or custom home - all of these grades of construction have different levels of quality, that you need to keep in mind.

Top Factors to Consider Before Investing (Demographic)

- SCHOOL DISTRICT RATINGS
- CRIME RATE
- JOB GROWTH RATE
- EDUCATION LEVEL
- TYPES OF JOBS AVAILABLE (OCCUPATIONS)

- GENDER
- AGE
- ANNUAL INCOME
- MARITAL STATUS
- LIVING STATUS (HOMEOWNERS OR RENTERS)

THE NUMBERS : DUE DILIGENCE

Performing your due diligence is the process of doing your initial research on the property, the market where it's located, and verifying the numbers before making your investment. Not every opportunity is a good opportunity, hence the importance of knowing and understanding Key Financial Investment Metrics to determine whether it is a good investment or not (Real Estate Investing is all about the numbers). **Online Resources for Due Diligence:** Zillow, Redfin, WalkScore.com, School Digger, WeGoLook, Google Maps.

Bonus (ZI) Tip:

You will also incur selling costs when you are getting ready to sell your property (that include closing costs, staging costs, home warranty, termite letter) etc.

Key Acquisition Metrics (When Buying A Property)

PURCHASE PRICE (Includes Closing Costs)
This refers to how much you pay for the property

Closing Costs: The total costs associated with you buying the property (will include legal fees, title and escrow fees, title insurance, transfer taxes, and agent commissions)

REHAB COSTS (Includes Holding Costs)
This refers to how much it costs you to renovate the property.

Holding Costs (Carrying Costs): these are expenses you incur during your **renovation** period and they include: points + mortgage interest (if you have a loan), general contractor fees, taxes, insurance, utilities, HOA fees, maintenance, project management. **Rentals:** property management, vacancy expense, taxes, utilities, HOA, insurance, & maintenance costs.

RETAIL VALUE
This is the value of your property if it were fully renovated, with recent updates and no repairs needed, what it would sell for on the open market. This is found by doing what is called a **(CMA - Comparable Market Analysis)** of recently sold homes in the area within a 0.5-mile radius of your subject property (with a similar bedroom / bathroom / sqft / lot size/year build) to your property

MARKET RENT
The metric that measures on average how much your property would garner in monthly rent based on similar rental properties to yours in the area and what they are currently being rented out for. (Visit zillow.com or rentometer.com to find this)

THE NUMBERS : DUE DILIGENCE

Key Investment Analysis Metrics

In real estate investing, you make your money when you buy. What this statement means is that you must buy the property at the RIGHT price right from the beginning in other to see a positive gain in the future from your investment. During your Due Diligence Period, get an appraisal & inspection reports, review surveys and any architectural plans if available, if the property is rented out - review the rent roll report that the owner should have about the tenant's payment history. Take into account all costs that will be associated with the investment (maintenance, taxes, insurance, utilities, etc.)

✓ INTERNAL RATE OF RETURN (IRR)

Represents the average annual % return over the lifetime of an investment **(or for the entire timeframe you own it)**, for each dollar you have invested. IRR compares multiple cash-flows of the same investment distributed at different yearly periods and is the total interest earned on the capital you invest. A Higher IRR isn't always better, this formula does have it's limitiations and shouldn't be used as the ONLY metric to analyze an investment. IRR can be found using **Microsoft excel or a financial calculator**

✓ RETURN ON INVESTMENT (ROI)

This is the ratio between the profits & costs of an investment expressed as a % (measures the profitability of investment based on your total gain (net profit) divided by total costs towards that investment) (Example: You made $50k NET Profit on a flip, your total costs: purchase price, renovation costs, closing costs, etc. were $150k - then your ROI = $50K/$150K = 33% ROI (this example assumes you financed the entire transaction all cash - no loan)

If you financed the deal (and only put 20% down (of purchase price), then your ROI would be 71% in this same scenario - because $20k downpayment + (repair costs + closing costs = $50k) = a new total cost of $70k (then divide original $50k NET Profit / $70k Total Cost

ROI on Financed Deal = 71%

Great Formula for Flips / Renovations

✓ CASH ON CASH RETURNS (COCR)

If you took out a loan for your rental property investment then this is the method you use to calculate your (ROI). It essentially is an equity invested **"cash-out-of-pocket analysis"** of your investment relative to your (Before Tax Cashflow). This ratio doesn't tell us about the "Profit" of an investment, rather it focuses on the rate of return of cash-flow the property will yield during a given an operational period.

Annual Income: NOI - Debt Service (annual mortgage & interest payments)
COCR Formula: Annual Income / Total Cash Invested (Equity Invested)

EX: You put down 20% on a house that costs $100k (that's $20k + you spend $10k in closing costs + $20k to renovate it, **you're all in at $50k of your own cash**) You then decide to rent it our for $2000/month. Your annual gross income is $24,000/year, your annual mortgage payment = ($400/mo x 12) = $4800
$24,000 - $4800 = $19,200 (Annual Income)

COCR Formula: $19,200 / $50,000 = 38%
COCR = 38%
Use this formula primarily for rentals (Not Flips)

THE NUMBERS : DUE DILIGENCE

Key Investment Analysis Metrics

The 3 key metrics as a landlord you always need to be aware of are your Net Operating Income (NOI), your Capitalization Rate (Cap Rate), and your Cash-Flow.

✅ NET OPERATING INCOME (NOI)

This metric is used to evaluate the profitability of an income-producing asset on a per-year basis. It is found by taking your Gross Annual Rental Income and subtracting your operating expenses from that #. **Operating Expenses (OE)** include Vacancy & Credit losses, Repairs & Maintenance (R&M), Property Taxes, Utilities, Insurance, Property Management.

Note: Annual Debt Service (Mortgage + Interest) are NOT calculated into Operating Expenses, because this is a financing cost specific to the investor exclude them **(This cost is calculated in CASHFLOW)**

Example: Gross Income: $14,400 - Vacancy 5% (of gross income) = $720 + $0 Other Income = Net Rental Income = $13,680
$13,680 is your total operating income and you subtract it by the operating expenses listed above (lets assume all together your OE are $7500), then
Your NOI = $13,680 - $7500 = $6180

$6180 = NOI

✅ CAP RATE

The rate of return expected to be generated by a rental real estate property and measures the risk associated with an investment.

CAP RATE Formula: NOI divided by Market Value

Example: $6180 / $100,000 property = 6% ROI

✅ CASH-FLOW

Cash-flow is essentially found using the same exact formula as Net Operating Income, the only difference is that once you have subtracted your operating expenses from your Annual Income, you THEN subtract your Annual Debt Service from your NOI.

Cashflow Formula: NOI - Debt Service

So if we used the same example as before, let's take our NOI of $6180 and assume our debt service (mortgage & interest payments for the year was $250/month, which equals $3000/yr)

Cashflow = $6180 - $3000 = $3180

Note: this is your **BTCF (Before Tax Cashflow)**

THE NUMBERS : DUE DILIGENCE

General Investment Guidelines

Investing is all about knowing your numbers and what they mean relative to your investment goals. These guidelines are here to help you as a guide to let you know whether or not you are entering a good deal, but there are a lot more factors to be considered than these guidelines. There are always unexpected market factors that would affect the outcome of each of these rules that a good real estate investment advisor would disclose to you.

THE (70%) RULE - "The Acquisition Ratio"

This is essentially the ideal **"Acquisition Ratio"** for all flips you intend on buying. The rule states you should pay no more than 70% of the **(After Repair Value)** minus repair cost. The terms ARV & Retail Value can be used interchangeably

For Example:
023 Main St, Atlanta Ga
ARV (Retail Value) = $200,000
Repair Cost = $50,000

Your Buy (Acquisition) price would be
$200,000 x 70% (minus) $50,000

= $90,000 (you should pay no more than $90,000 for this deal)

THE (1%) RULE (Rent to Value Ratio)

An easy way to know if you're getting a good rental deal, calculating how much your rents should be, and how much you should pay for a rental. The rule states that your monthly rent should be (equal to or greater than) 1% of your total purchase price (including repairs).

Example: Purchase Price: $90,000
Repairs: $10,000
Total Price: $100,000 (1% of $100k is $1,000)

Your Monthly Market Rent To Your Tenant Should Be A Minimum of $1,000 (or greater)

THE (50%) RULE)

This is simply a quick and easy way to calculate the **Net Operating Income** of a rental property. It states that you will only retain 50% of your gross rental income after accounting for your expenses - vacancy, management, insurance, maintenance, taxes, repairs, utilities)

For Example A Rental You Own
market rent = $1200 / month.

$1200 x 12 (months) = $14,400
$14,400 = **Your Gross Yearly Income**

$14,400 x 50% = $7200 **NOI**
So you should expect somewhere around $7200 in Net Income after expenses for this rental you own.

THE NUMBERS : DUE DILIGENCE

APPROACHES TO PROPERTY VALUATION

The main difference between a commercial and residential property is how their values are assessed - with commercial assets, their values are based solely on the income the property brings in (net operating income) & cap rate (noi/price) whereas, a residential property its value is based upon what is called a comparative market analysis, income approach, or cost basis approach).

✓ COMPARABLE MARKET ANALYSIS

Analyzing the average of 3-6 recently SOLD comparable **(COMPS)** properties within a 0.5 to 1 mile radius of your subject property (with similar - bedrooms, bathrooms, square feet, lot size, and year build

Use this approach when you are renovating. wholesaling, or wholetailing.

✓ INCOME APPROACH

Calculating the value of an asset based on the cash-flow it generates (usually done by calculating Net Operating Income divided by your Purchase Price) = **Cap Rate** - this approach is great for rentals and commercial apartments.

✓ COST BASIS APPROACH (for tax purposes)

Cost of property (or land) + construction expenses (minus) depreciation - this approach is good for new construction developments

Note: if it is a property you already own that is developed keep track of all expenses and renovations you make to calculate your **"adjusted cost bases"**

FINANCING YOUR INVESTMENT

There are two primary ways to finance a real estate investment deal (usually in the form of **debt (loan)** or **equity (cash)** or a variation of both.

EQUITY FINANCING EXAMPLES

- Friends and Family
- 401k/Self Directed IRA
- Your Savings
- Trust Fund

DEBT FINANCING EXAMPLES

- Hard Money Lender (can get very costly)
- Conventional Mortgage Lender
- Home Equity Line Of Credit (HELOC Loan)
- Business and Personal lines of credit
- Whole Life Insurance Policy

CASH INVESTOR TIP

"I recommend working towards saving or having access to at least anywhere from $100k-$300,000 in cash if you want to be a serious all cash buyer in a market like Atlanta Georgia which we are currently investing in at Zirow Invest. (other markets will vary)"

- Victor E. Bomi

Debt Financing (Your Alternative to Cash)

Hard Money & Conventional Mortgage Lenders will be your primary
source for debt financing and you will need the following

"You can typically
expect to pay 12-
21% in interest
rates to hard
money lenders"

WHAT YOU NEED FOR FINANCING

- A GOOD CREDIT SCORE (680 & ABOVE)
- INCOME & BANK STATEMENTS (3-6 MONTHS BACK)
- CASH RESERVES
- DOWN PAYMENT (33% of Median Home Values In Your Target Market)

3 KEY FACTORS LENDERS CONSIDER TO FINANCE YOU

- DEBT TO INCOME Ratio (DTI)
- CREDIT SCORE
- LOAN TO VALUE RATIO (LTV)

Debt Financing (DEBT TO INCOME)

DTI measures the size of your monthly debt burden relative to the size of your monthly pay - helps lenders decide if you can really afford another loan.

DTI Formula

Current Recurring Debt Obligations (monthly)

Gross Income Monthly

Key Points

- The **max you can have is 43%**, any ratio higher than that suggests to the lender that you would be a highly risky borrower

- The ideal DTI for a borrower is **36% or less**

Debt Financing (CREDIT SCORES)

A 3 digit system, used by lenders to determine how likely you are to repay a debt. They **Range from 300-850** - the lower the riskier you are, the higher the less risky you are to the lender. (generally, most lenders want to see **at least a 680** score but you should **aim to have 740 and up** as that is what is considered "very good credit" if you're going the route of financing your investments.

You can check your score at myFICO.com, AnnualCreditScore.com, and FreeCreditScore.com

What is a good FICO SCORE?

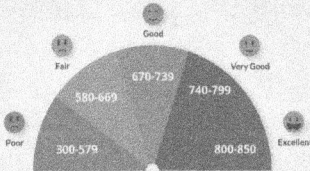

- Poor 300-579
- Fair 580-669
- Good 670-739
- Very Good 740-799
- Excellent 800-850

Source: MyFICO

lendingtree

Adding Up the FICO Score

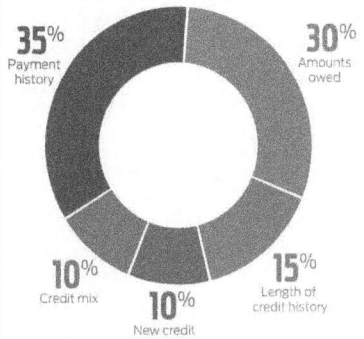

- **35%** Payment history
- **30%** Amounts owed
- **15%** Length of credit history
- **10%** New credit
- **10%** Credit mix

SOURCE: MyFICO

Debt Financing (IMPROVING YOUR CREDIT SCORE)

BONUS TIP: a good credit utilization ratio is less than 30 percent. This means you're using less than 30 percent of the total credit available to you.

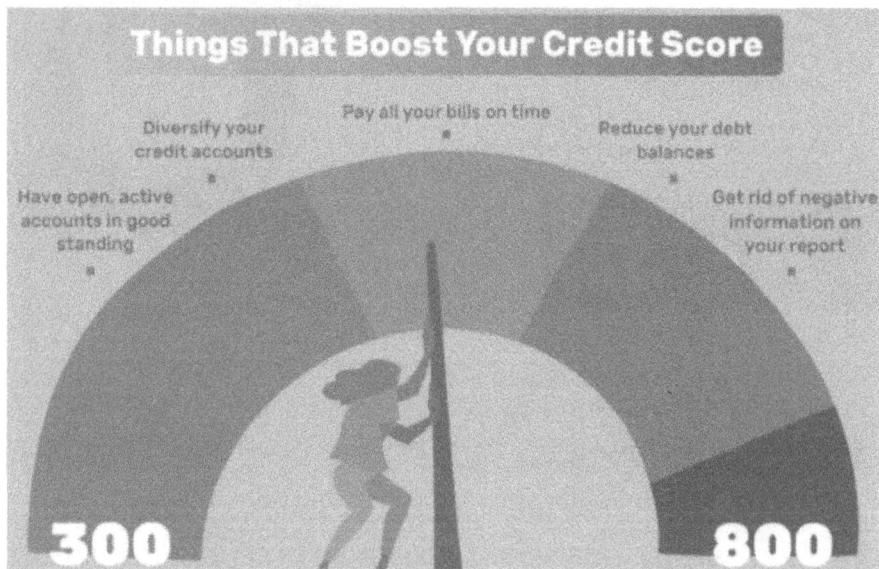

Things That Boost Your Credit Score

Diversify your credit accounts

Pay all your bills on time

Reduce your debt balances

Have open, active accounts in good standing

Get rid of negative information on your report

300   800

Debt Financing (LOAN TO VALUE - LTV)

A loan-to-value (LTV) ratio is the number that shows the difference between what you owe on your mortgage and the value of your property. (The more you bring to the table in terms of a down payment - the lower your LTV will be, which makes you a less risky and more stable borrower to the lender - ideally a good rule of thumb for most lenders is to lend at **no more than 80% LTV to any borrower**) - LTV determines your interest rate as well as your loan type, the lower your LTV, the better deal / lower interest rate the lender charges you.

Loan-to-Value Ratio Formula and Calculation

Home buyers can easily calculate the LTV ratio on their home.

$$LTV\,ratio = \frac{MA}{APV}$$

where:

MA = Mortgage Amount

APV = Appraised Property Value

BONUS TIP: Fannie Mae's HomeReady and Freddie Mac's Home Possible mortgage programs for low-income borrowers allow an LTV ratio of 97% (3% down payment) but require mortgage insurance until the LTV ratio falls to 80%.

Debt Financing (UNDERSTANDING LTV)

How To Calculate LTV

LTV is calculated by dividing the loan amount by the appraised value of the property.
Here's an example that illustrates how LTV is calculated.
Loan amount/property value = LTV
Appraised property value: $200,000
Loan amount: $180,000
$180,000/$200,000 = 0.9
LTV: 90%

How Does A Down Payment Impact Your LTV?

When buying a home, you can lower your LTV by increasing your down payment.
Here's an example of how a larger down payment can decrease your LTV.
Appraised property value: $200,000
Down payment: $50,000
Loan amount: $150,000
$150,000/$200,000 = 0.75
LTV: 75%

How Does Your Equity Impact Your LTV?

As you make mortgage payments and your property value increases, you're building equity, lowering your LTV.
Here's an example of how equity can impact your LTV.
Property value: $200,000
Loan balance: $125,000
Equity: $75,000
$125,000/$200,000 = 0.625
LTV: 63%

How Does A Decrease In Property Value Impact The LTV?

Your property can decrease in value if the home is not maintained over time, or if the housing market drops dramatically. When this happens, your LTV rises.

Here's an example of how a decreased property value can affect your LTV.
Original purchase price: $200,000
Property value: $150,000
Loan balance: $175,000
$175,000/$150,000 = 1.166
LTV: 117%

When your home loan balance is higher than the value of your home, it's referred to as being **"underwater."** This means you owe the lender more than the value of your home, and it's a situation you want to avoid by paying your mortgage consistently and researching the value of comparable homes in the same area.

SOURCE: QUICKENLOANS.COM

Debt Financing (ALTERNATIVE LOAN OPTIONS)

	Conventional	FHA	USDA	VA
What it is	This is your 'plain vanilla' mortgage made by a bank to a buyer with no third party involved	FHA loans are insured by the Federal Housing Administration (part of HUD).	USDA loans are guaranteed by USDA for homes in areas deemed 'rural'	VA loans are guaranteed by the Department of Veteran Affairs for eligible Veterans
Pros	• Lower monthly mortgage insurance, making the overall payment lower • No mortgage insurance needed if 20% down • If mortgage insurance needed, it can go away once buyer has 20% equity • property standards not as picky • Less paperwork involved	• More flexibility with bruised or newer credit, limited savings or tighter debt-to-income • Down payment can be gifted from a family member • Interest rate is often lower than that for a conventional loan • Lower minimum down payment needed than with conventional (3.5% vs. 5%)	• No down payment needed • Monthly mortgage insurance is less expensive, making the overall payment lower • In some situations, the cost for repairs can be rolled into the loan • Interest rate is often lower than for a conventional loan	• No down payment needed • No monthly mortgage insurance • VA Funding fee can be waived if Veteran has over 10% disability • Interest rate is often lower than for a conventional loan
Cons	• Holds buyer to a higher standard in terms of credit, savings and debt-to-income • Larger down payment needed (5% minimum) • Interest rate and monthly mortgage insurance is more expensive with lower credit scores	• Monthly mortgage insurance is typically more expensive and it stays for the life of the loan • FHA charges a 1.75% upfront fee (rolled into the loan balance) • The property needs to meet a higher standard than needed for conventional loans • More paperwork is involved	• Only homes in eligible areas can be financed with USDA mortgages • USDA needs to review all files which often delays the closing process • The home needs to meet minimum property standards set by USDA that are more stringent than some other loan types	• Property needs to meet a slightly higher standard • Seller has to pay for certain fees that typically are paid for by buyer (termite inspection and title company closing fee) • More paperwork is involved

Navigating Taxes In Real Estate Investing

Key Taxes You Pay

1. Property Taxes

2. Capital Gains Tax

1. Income Tax

Property Taxes: These are taxes that are based on the assessed value of your property that you have to pay to the state in which your property is located in (usually a %, that varies from state to state)

Capital Gains: is the profit you make when you sell an appreciated asset like property. If you hold on to the property for less than a year, then it is considered a short-term gain - which is then taxed as ordinary income at a rate up to 37% whereas if you own it for more than a year it is considered a long-term capital gain and your capital gains tax would be anywhere from 0-20% depending on income.

Navigating Taxes In Real Estate Investing

Rental Income Tax Breakdown

A rental property is classified by IRS definition as a property in which in a given year, you rent out for 15 days or more (and or live in for 14 days or less than 10% of the days it was rented) and gain income from leasing it out to another individual or company.

Rental income is reported on the IRS "Schedule E" form and taxed as ordinary income (based on your tax bracket and filing status), and also based on your accounting method "most people use cash-basis" but some businesses use the "accrual method - which counts income when it's earned not when it's received" As a result of the new tax reforms in the country, Rental Income also now qualify for the (QBI) "Qualified Business Income" deduction that allows for you to deduct up to 20% off your taxable income.

You especially have to be very organized and keep a spreadsheet that contains detailed records of your income and expenses) - a good CPA/accountant is important to help you simplify this process.

Navigating Taxes In Real Estate Investing (Tax Deductions)

One key benefit of real estate investing is the ability to deduct your expenses, in addition to pass through deductions, you can also deduct the following expenses:

- Depreciation
- Property Taxes
- Insurance
- Property Management Fees
- Mortgage Interest (not the mortgage)
- Legal Fees

- Advertising Fees
- Closing Costs
- Utilities
- HOA Fees
- Home Office Expenses
- Travel and Mileage Expenses

General Rule: any expense you incur from maintaining and operating your property can be deducted

Depreciation is usually your largest deduction (if you are a rental investor) and is the process of deducting the cost of an asset that has a useful life of one year or more. In order for an asset to qualify for depreciation it needs to have a useful life that can be "quantifiable" i.e. rental property, machinery, etc.

The IRS guidelines for the useful life for residential rental properties is 27.5 years, and for a commercial property 39 years. (you are required to own the property for over a year to qualify for depreciation deduction & land can't be depreciated). Your cost basis - is the amount of money you paid for the property (including any mortgage debt, legal cost while you acquired the property, recording fees, title insurance costs, and transfer taxes) minus the value of the land it is built on.

Cost basis can also be adjusted over time as you renovate the property, to include your renovation costs as well - this is called an **"adjusted basis"**

Navigating Taxes In Real Estate Investing - Deeper Dive Into Depreciation

HOW TO CALCULATE DEPRECIATION EXPENSE

If you own your rental property for the entire calendar year, calculating depreciation is simple.
For residential rental properties, take your cost basis (or adjusted cost basis, if applicable) and divide it by 27.5.
Another way to understand this formula is: for each full year you own a rental property, you are allowed to depreciate 3.636% of your cost basis each year.

EXAMPLE

If your cost basis in a rental property is $200,000, your annual depreciation expense is $7,273.
For a commercial property, divide your cost basis by 39.
This gives you a 2.564% depreciation expense for each full year you own the property.
It's more complicated when you own the property for only part of a calendar year.
This generally occurs in the years when you buy and sell a property.
In these cases, you can prorate the depreciation based on how many months of the year you used the property to generate rental income.

SOURCE: Fool.com

Here are the most common divisions of tax basis for a rental property, followed by explanations of the different methods of depreciation that generally apply:

Type of Property	Method of Depreciation	Useful Life in Years
Land	Not allowed	N/A
Residential rental real estate (buildings or structures and structural components)	Straight line	27.5
Nonresidential rental real estate	Straight line	39
Shrubbery, fences, etc.	150% declining balance	15
Furniture or appliances	200% declining balance	5

SOURCE: TurboTax.com

Navigating Taxes In Real Estate Investing

Lowering Your Tax Rate + 1031 Exchange Deeper Dive

Lowering Your Tax Rate

- Using a 1031 Exchange

- Setting up a self-directed IRA (to invest tax-free)

- Reduce your taxable income by setting up a (tax deferred) 401k and making the maximum yearly contribution

- Own the asset for more than a year

- Tax-loss harvesting (timing your capital gains tax with your capital loss deduction - to offset and reduce your capital gains)

- Home improvement expenses you make over the years

- Donate the asset to a tax-exempt charity

1031 Exchange Deeper Dive

A 1031 exchange gets its name from Section 1031 of the U.S. Internal Revenue Code, which allows you to avoid paying capital gains taxes when you sell an investment property and reinvest the proceeds from the sale within certain time limits in a property or properties of like kind and equal or greater value.

★ SECTION CONCLUSION

KEY TAKEAWAYS: The key to being a successful real estate investor is to "Buy Right" - you make your money when you buy, not when you sell - so you always want to be targeting Discounted Properties (never pay retail - that has been one of the guiding principles at our company that has helped us be successful)

Be precise and clear on what it is you want to accomplish in real estate and why - cashflow goal? income goal? profit goal? # doors / units goal? Fire Your Boss #? - get specific about your #s, a system to support these goals, be sure to get connected with our real estate investment managers that can help you put together a comprehensive plan to accomplish your investment goals. Real Estate Investing takes a lot of work and time to be successful, but the key to being successful is having a realistic and comprehensive investment plan and having a good team around you to simplify the process for you.

KEY MISTAKES TO AVOID

- Being too optimistic about resale-value
- Using the wrong investment strategy in a particular market
- Overpaying for a property
- Underestimating renovation cost
- Miscalculating renovation timeline
- Lacking cash reserves
- Bad agents who are only worried about a commission and selling you a property (and not your returns)
- Bad contractors
- Investing with emotion
- Not setting up your corporate structure correctly for tax and legal purposes
- Trying to go at it alone instead of leveraging the experience of someone who has successfully invested in real estate.

SECTION CONCLUSION

Getting started investing in real estate can always be overwhelming in the beginning but with the right team, foundation and strategies in place, you can do it successfully, this section was all about giving you the foundational knowledge needed to get started investing in real estate, **in the next section we are going to be discussing the Covid19 situation, how it is affecting the real estate market, and what we are doing to successfully navigate through it.**

RESOURCES FOR YOU

1. ESTATE INVESTMENT ACTION PLAN by Zirow Invest
2. SPREADSHEET INVESTMENT CALCULATOR

Visit: zirowinvest.com/resources

I would like to hear your feedback from this section, and if you found value in it - email: info@victorbomi.com or dm me on Instagram @VictorBomi and **enjoy the next section.**

COVID19 EFFECTS ON AMERICAN REAL ESTATE MARKET

Introduction & Context

The Coronavirus came out of nowhere and has disrupted the world and we won't really know the full effects this virus will have on global markets until a few years later after it has passed. As investors, we can't control the market but we can adjust to it.

Big Picture Outlook: To fully understand the extent of the economic fallout we can take a look at how this situation compares to the other major economic downturns that happened in this country: The 08 Financial Crisis & Great Depression.

COVID19 EFFECTS ON AMERICAN REAL ESTATE MARKET

Covid19 vs. 2008 Financial Crisis

08 Crisis Unemployment - peaked right around 10%.
Covid19 Unemployment - As of today, the current unemployment rate is 20%, via FORTUNE.COM

08 Crisis Market Decline - caused by the default of subprime mortgage loans (higher risk borrowers), high speculation, over-valued properties & collateralized debt obligations.
Covid19 Market Decline - will likely come from the rate of job losses, tenants defaulting on rent, landlords defaulting on mortgages.

08 Crisis National Debt - $10 Trillion
2020 National Debt - $24 Trillion and counting

COVID19 - IMPACT ON PROPERTY VALUES

In the 2008 Financial Crisis property values fell anywhere from **10-30%** depending on what part of the country you were in) we don't expect to see property values decline as sharply as they did then, but they definitely will as a result of property owners willing to take reduced offers in exchange for quicker closings (to build their cash reserves)

Study on prior pandemic effects on the housing market, sales are largely what is most impacted by a pandemic, property values will decrease too but - only slightly initially (Source: Zillow.com)

COVID19 EFFECTS ON AMERICAN REAL ESTATE MARKET

Covid19 vs. 1929 Great Depression

Great Depression Unemployment - peaked at 25%
Covid19 Unemployment - 20% as of today

Stock Market & Banks (Great Depression) - The catalyst for the great depression of 1930 was caused by the stock market crash of 1929 & major bank failures
Stock Market & Banks (Covid19 Crisis) - the housing market is not positively correlated to the US stock market, mainly because housing is an essential need and not just an investment, and most banks are going to receive bailouts (from $350B Covid19 Bailout Package) to avoid massive bank failures

COVID19 EFFECTS ON AMERICAN REAL ESTATE MARKET

The Opportunity

Anytime a recession happens, there is always a massive transfer of wealth & some people end up on the winning side, while others end up on the losing side - you have an opportunity to decide which side you want to be on

COVID19 EFFECTS ON AMERICAN REAL ESTATE INDUSTRY

KEY REAL ESTATE SECTORS AFFECTED

- Hotels

- Air BNBs (Short-Term Rentals)

- Commercial Real Estate (Office Spaces & Retail)

EFFECTS OF COVID19 IN THE INDUSTRY

- Residential Supply Chain Disruption: (if you're a developer or rehabber who relies on sourcing your materials out of state, from states under a mandatory shut-down like California, you now have to spend more for local material suppliers.

- The shut-down of both commercial and residential construction job sites in some States

- Lenders have tightened up their criteria - requiring a higher down payment and increased credit score requirements to secure investment loans - as a result, a Large % of buyers have been taken out of the market

- Some sellers have decided to take their homes off the market, while others are trying to sell as soon as possible to have some cash reserves

- It is now a buyers market and no longer a seller's market (which means better deals for you as an investor)

- There will be a reduction in home values as a result of there being less demand for homes

- As more homeowners lose their jobs and default on their loans, people will begin to downsize and there will be a rise in distressed sales, foreclosures and short sales

PIVOTING & ADJUSTING

How We Are Adjusting

1. Certain aspects of our acquisition process has gone virtual (virtual showings, virtual mail away closings) - due to social distancing requirements by government

2. Most of our meetings are now held via ZOOM, and contracts signed via Docusign

2. We are being more creative with our deals and contracts (added a Covid19 clause) to give us more time to perform our due diligence

3. With the massive amount of opportunities coming, we are raising more capital to invest in deals & opening up more investor joint venture opportunities

4. We are being more conservative with our #s (our all-in acquisition ratio is now between 40-60%, as opposed to the traditional 70% rule, and we are discounting retail values by 10-15%)

5. We are NOT buying heavy renovation projects, sticking only to light cosmetic remodels

6. Reducing cost and being more cost-efficient with our day to day operations to maximize every dollar

7. We are negotiating much better deals for ourselves and our investors due to the market uncertainty

8. We are focused on acquiring properties that give us MULTIPLE EXIT OPTIONS (Wholesale, Wholetail, Rent It Out, or Renovate)

What You Can Do

1. Maintain a positive mindset & surround yourself with people who have a positive outlook on this situation

2. Build Your War Chest (Your Cash Reserves) to be prepared for the buying opportunities that are coming

3. Sell any property assets you have right now that may be at risk - while the market is still relatively at the top (and put yourself in a better liquid position)

4. Diversify your Investment Portfolio

5. Focus on Cashflow (look for passive income or rental opportunities)

6. Go Virtual (look for ways to invest and operate virtually)

7. Create relationships with REO Agents & Asset managers (who have access to bank deals - due to the upcoming rise in foreclosures and short sales)

SECTION CONCLUSION

Stay Strong. Stay Positive.

KEY TAKEAWAYS: ADAPTING is the key to success in a changing real estate market, focus on building your cash reserves to capitalize on the opportunities in the market that will be coming in the next 6-9 months, the real estate market is resilient and always bounces back so be sure that you are prepared to take advantage of the opportunities that will come about in the market.

KEY MISTAKES TO AVOID

- Doing major developments during this economic climate
- over-paying for a property
- over-leveraging yourself - don't take on too much debt in this uncertain environment
- Having a negative or defeated mindset because of the virus

KEY RESOURCES FOR YOU

1. Free PDF Guide by J Scott on Investing In A Recession Economy

zirowinvest.com/resources

I would like to hear from you, be sure to get in touch with me and let me know your thoughts on the book if you enjoyed it share it with a few friends who may find it interesting as well.
(email: info@victorbomi.com) | Be sure to follow @ZirowInvest & @VictorBomi on instagram/twitter

Special Thank You

I just want to extend my thanks to you for taking the time to read my first literary work. I put a lot of time into making sure I was able to provide as much value as I can to you with this book. Real Estate Investing doesn't have to be complicated, and after reading this book you will be on the right track towards creating financial freedom for yourself. I dedicate this book to my family and friends, and I appreciate all of your support. Be sure to share this book with 1 or 2 people who you know are also interested in investing in real estate, cheers to your success and I wish you the very best.

-Victor E. Bomi, CEO, Zirow Invest, LLC.

START WITH ZIROW

schedule a consultation via zirowinvest.com/consultation if you're interested in investing in real estate.

www.ingramcontent.com/pod-product-compliance
Lightning Source LLC
Chambersburg PA
CBHW021916190326
41519CB00008B/804